The Code of the Samurai

The Code of the Samurai

A translation of
Daidōji Yūzan's *Budō Shoshinshū*

by A. L. Sadler

CHARLES E. TUTTLE COMPANY
Rutland, Vermont & Tokyo, Japan

Published by the Charles E. Tuttle Company, Inc.
of Rutland, Vermont & Tokyo, Japan with editorial offices
at Suido 1-chome, 2-6 , Bunkyo-ku, Tokyo 112
by special arrangement with the heirs of A. L. Sadler
and The Japan Foundation, ARK Mori Building, 1-12-32
Akasaka, Minato-ku, Tokyo 107, Japan

This English translation of *Budō Shoshinshū*
was first published in 1941 by Kokusai Bunka Shinkokai
under the title *The Beginner's Book of Bushido*

LCC Card No. 87-51232
ISBN 0-8048-1535-6

First Tuttle Edition, 1988
Eleventh printing, 1995

PRINTED IN SINGAPORE

CONTENTS

PUBLISHER'S FOREWORD

This remarkable book, the translation of Daidōji Yūzan's sixteenth-century text for young samurai, is one of the most authentic records ever produced of Japanese chivalry, or Bushido.

First published in English in 1941, *The Code of the Samurai* presents the "honor system" of the Japanese warrior in a series of straightforward rules. Although out of print for many years, it has retained its reputation as an accurate exposition of a samurai's practical and moral training, and remains a valuable guide to the Japanese school of thought and life.

We would like to extend our thanks to the heirs of A. L. Sadler and to The Japan Foundation, for granting us the permission to reprint this book. Acknowledgments are also due to Satoshi Nakamura and Takako Katsu of The Japan Foundation, who assisted in bringing *The Code of the Samurai* back into print.

Tokyo, 1987

TRANSLATOR'S NOTE

The historical documents that illustrate the main concepts connected with Bushido* or Japanese chivalry are, in earlier days, the various accounts of the activities of the warrior in war and peace, and later on the House Laws and sets of maxims drawn up by the great feudal lords or sometimes by lesser personages. Among the latter is this textbook for young samurai which purports to lay down what was required of them in the latter half of the sixteenth and early seventeenth century. The author

*The word "Bushido," like "Samurai," has become a loan-word in English and is explained as "The national spirit of Japan, especially the military spirit, traditional chivalry as of the old Samurai class." Its literal meaning is "the Way of the Warrior" and it is found in Japanese first in the late sixteenth century, e.g. in the legacy of Torii Mototada (1539–1600), and elsewhere. Some European writers, following Chamberlain, have maintained that both the word and what it signifies are inventions of the Meiji period intended to fortify national sentiment and unknown before. The currency of the word in the West is no doubt chiefly due to the book called *Bushido* published in 1899 by Dr. Nitobe, whence the careless statement in a largely circulated popular American work on the thought of the Orient, "Bushido, a word invented by Inazo Nitobe."

was an expert in the military arts and a prominent writer of those days, and since he lived to the age of ninety-two under the rule of six shoguns from Iemitsu to Yoshimune—he was twelve when Iemitsu died and Yoshimune had been shogun for fifteen years when he himself died—he had known the atmosphere of the early Tokugawa period as it was only a decade after the death of Ieyasu, and had lived to see the splendor of the Genroku age under the luxurious and eccentric Tsunayoshi. As a retainer of the Tokugawa house he was familiar with the work and teachings of the sage Mitsukuni, Lord of Mito, and was also the pupil of Yamaga Sokō, another eminent writer on Bushido and seventeen years his senior. He had witnessed the heroic example of the Forty-Seven Loyal Rōnin of Akō, whose leader Ōishi Yoshio was another pupil of Sokō, and also the ruin of more than one feudal lord owing to domestic trouble caused by the machinations of evil retainers. He was the contemporary also of the great scholar Arai Hakuseki, whose well-known autobiography gives a picture of a samurai family very much according to his ideal. Few can have been better qualified to expatiate on this subject, and his advice as to what the samurai should avoid is very clearly based on the falling away from the austerity and simplicity of the "days of old" that he had in his later days experienced and which the Shogun Yoshimune with his principle of "back to Ieyasu" tried so earnestly to correct. And his work gives a very clear and lively account of Bushido as he knew it, perhaps more succinct than can be found elsewhere, while more detailed than such sets of articles as the "Hundred Rules" of Takeda Shingen or of Ieyasu. Moreover, it is written entirely from the point of view of the retainer and not of the lord. For this reason I have used the word "samurai" in it instead of "bushi," which is not so familiar to readers of English, though it is more comprehensive as meaning the military man or warrior and therefore including the daimyo, or feudal lord, which the term samurai does not. "Samurai" is an expression of respectable antiquity incidentally, and a pure Japanese one, first used in the sense of military retainer in the tenth century, and adopted in the late twelfth century by the Kamakura military government as the official designation of the War Department or Samurai-dokoro.

Daidōji Yūzan Shigesuke was of a distinguished samurai family claiming descent from the Taira clan through Taira Korehira (10th cent.). His ancestor in the fifth generation was Shigetoki, elder brother of Ise Shinkurō Nagauji, who became famous as Hōjō Sōun, lord of Odawara, and one of the outstanding warrior administrators of his day. Shigetoki took the name of Daidōji from the village where he retired. His grandson Masashige committed suicide when Odawara was taken by Hideyoshi in 1590, and his son Naoshige became a vassal of Tokugawa Hidetada and fought valiantly at the siege of Osaka, helping to rally the Shogun's troops when they were badly shaken by the desperate charge of the garrison. Yūzan's father, Shigehisa, was a vassal of Tokugawa Tadateru, Ieyasu's sixth son and younger brother of Hidetada, who became suspect, lost his fief, and was retired. Yūzan seems to have followed his father as his retainer for a time, but meanwhile he studied and became an orthodox Confucian scholar and expert in military affairs and took a position as military adviser to Lord Matsudaira of Aizu. He then retired to Iwabuchi in Musashi, but later on went to live in the household of Matsudaira, Echizen no Kami, chief of the Kamon or direct relative houses of the Shogun. Evidently he practiced what he recommended, for he is described as a pattern of loyalty, self-control, and equanimity. He was also a verse writer of some note. As an author he is well known for the *Iwabuchi Yawa* or "Evening Chats at Iwabuchi," a series of anecdotes about Tokugawa Ieyasu arranged in chronological order, and the perhaps more familiar *Ochiboshū,* a history of Ieyasu and his connections and successors, and of the city and castle of Edo which they built. He also wrote the *Taishōden* or "Records of Great Commanders" and the *Goshinron* or "Essays on Five Vassals."

CHAPTER I

Introduction

One who is a samurai must before all things keep constantly in mind, by day and by night, from the morning when he takes up his chopsticks to eat his New Year's breakfast to Old Year's night when he pays his yearly bills, the fact that he has to die. That is his chief business. If he is always mindful of this, he will be able to live in accordance with the paths of Loyalty and Filial Duty, will avoid myriads of evils and adversities, keep himself free from disease and calamity and moreover enjoy a long life. He will also be a fine personality with many admirable qualities. For existence is impermanent as the dew of evening and the hoarfrost of morning, and particularly uncertain is the life of the warrior, and if he thinks he can console himself with the idea of eternal service to his lord or unending devotion to his relatives, something may well happen to make him neglect his duty to his lord and forget what he owes to his family. But if he determines simply to live for today and take no thought for the morrow, so that when he stands before his lord to receive his commands he thinks of it as his last appearance and when he looks on the faces of his relatives he feels that he will never see them again, then will his duty and regard for both of them be completely sincere, while his mind will be in accord with the path of loyalty and filial duty.

But if he does not keep death in mind he will be careless and liable to be indiscreet and say things that offend others and an argument ensues, and though, if no notice is taken, it may be settled, if there is a rebuke, it may end in a quarrel. Then, if he goes strolling about pleasure resorts and seeing the sights in crowded places without any proper reserve, he may come up against some big fool and get into a quarrel before he knows it, and may even be killed and his lord's name brought into it and his parents and relations exposed to reproach.

And all this misfortune springs from his not remembering to keep death always in his thoughts. But one who does this whether he is speaking himself or answering others will carefully consider, as befits a samurai, every word he says and never launch out into useless argument. Neither will he allow anyone to entice him into unsuitable places where he may be suddenly confronted with an awkward situation, and thus he avoids evils and calamities. And both high and low, if they forget about

death, are very apt to take to unhealthy excess in
food and wine and women so that they die unex-
pectedly early from diseases of the kidneys and
spleen, and even while they live their illness makes
them of no use to anyone. But those who keep death
always before their eyes are strong and healthy while
young, and as they take care of their health and are
moderate in eating and drinking and avoid the paths
of women, being abstemious and moderate in all
things, they remain free from disease and live a long
and healthy life.

Then one who lives long in this world may de-
velop all sorts of desires and his covetousness may
increase so that he wants what belongs to others and
cannot bear to part with what is his own, becoming
in fact just like a mere tradesman. But if he is always
looking death in the face, a man will have little at-
tachment to material things and will not exhibit these
grasping and covetous qualities, and will become,
as I said before, a fine character. And speaking of
meditation on death, Yoshida Kenkō says in the
Tsurezure-Gusa of the monk Shinkai that he was
wont to sit all day long pondering on his latter end;
this is no doubt a very suitable attitude for a recluse
but by no means so for a warrior. For so he would
have to neglect his military duties and the way of
loyalty and filial piety, and he must on the contrary
be constantly busy with his affairs both public and
private. But whenever he has a little spare time to
himself and can be quiet he should not fail to revert

to this question of death and reflect carefully on it. Is it not recorded that Kusunoki Masashige adjured his son Masatsura to keep death always before his eyes? And all this is for the instruction of the youthful samurai.

Education

Since the samurai stands at the head of the three classes of society and has the duty of carrying on the administration, it is incumbent on him to be well educated and to have a wide knowledge of the reason of things. However, in the period of civil war, the young warrior went out to battle when he was fifteen or sixteen, so that he had to start his military education at twelve or thirteen. Since he had no time to sit down with a book or take up a writing brush, he was often quite illiterate. In fact, in these days there were a lot of samurai who could not write a single Chinese character. So whether through their own want of inclination or the faulty instruction of their parents, nothing was done about it, because their whole life was devoted exclusively to the Way of the Warrior. Now, however, the empire is at peace, and though one cannot exactly say that those born in samurai families are indifferent to military training, yet there is no question of their being forced to enter a warlike career at the age of fifteen or sixteen like the warrior of former days. So that at the age of seven or eight when he is growing up, a boy should be introduced to the Four Books, the Five Classics, and the Seven Texts and taught calligraphy so that he remembers how to write characters. Then, when he is fifteen or sixteen, he should be made to practice archery and horsemanship and all the other military arts, for that is the way that the samurai should bring up his sons in time of peace. There is no excuse for illiteracy in his case as there was in that of the warrior of the civil war period. And children are not to blame for lack of education either. It is entirely due to the neglect and incompetence of their parents who do not really know the way of affection for their children.

Filial Duty

One who is a samurai should base his conduct on a strong sense of filial duty. And however capable and clever and eloquent and handsome one may be born, if he is unfilial he is of no use at all. For Bushido, the

Way of the Warrior, requires a man's conduct to be correct in all points. For if there is no discrimination in all matters there will be no knowledge of what is right. And one who does not know what is right can hardly be called a samurai. Now he who has this complete insight realizes that his parents are the authors of his being and that he is part of their flesh and blood. And it is from the inclination to exalt this part which is ourselves that matters sometimes arise that lead us to slight the parental origin of it. This is want of discrimination of the order of cause and effect.

Now in rendering filial obligations to parents there are two varieties. The first is where the parent's disposition is honest and he educates his children with sincere kindliness and leaves them all his property, including an income above the average and weapons and horse furniture and household treasures, as well as arranging good marriages for them. When such a parent retires it is neither praiseworthy nor remarkable that his children should look after him and treat him with all consideration. Even toward a complete outsider, if he is an intimate friend and goes out of his way to be helpful to us, we feel very kindly disposed and do anything we can for him though it may be contrary to our own interests. How much deeper then must the bond of affection be where our parents are concerned? So, however much we do for them as children, we cannot but feel that however well we fulfill our filial duties it is never really quite adequate. And this is just the ordinary filial piety that is not anything remarkable. But if the parent is not kindly but old and crotchety and is always nagging, insisting that the household property belongs to him, who gives his children nothing, and without considering the scanty means of the family is always making all kinds of importunate demands for drink and food and clothes. And not only so but whenever he meets other people he says something to this effect, "This beastly son of mine is unfilial and so I have to put up with all sorts of discomfort. You have no idea what a bad time I have in my old age," thus giving his children a bad name among outsiders. Even such a cantankerous parent must be reverenced as a parent and his bad temper be appeased and his aged infirmities condoled with and regretted and that without showing any signs of annoyance. For exerting oneself to the utmost for such a parent is real filial piety. And a samurai who possesses this spirit when he enters the service of a lord will thoroughly understand the Way of Loyalty and will show it not only when his master is prosperous but also if he meets adversity, and will not leave his side when his hundred horsemen are reduced to ten and this ten to one, but will defend him to the last, regarding his life as nothing in carrying out a warrior's fealty. And so though the terms "parent" and "lord," "filial conduct" and "loyalty," are distinct, they are in no way different in meaning. There is a saying of the ancients, "Look for a loyal retainer among the filial"; and it is unreasonable to think that if a man is unfilial to his parents he can at the same time be loyal to his master. For if anyone is incapable of carrying out his filial duties to his parents from whom he sprung, it is very unlikely that he will give loyal service to a lord who is no relation, out of pure gratitude. When he enters a lord's service an unfilial son of this kind will be critical of any shortcoming of his master, and when he does not approve of anything he will throw off his allegiance and slip away at a critical moment or betray his lord by giving himself up to the enemy. There are examples of such disgraceful conduct in all periods and it is to be shunned with abhorrence.

Samurai Ordinances

In Bushido there are two ordinances and four sections. The two ordinances are the ordinary and the extraordinary, and the ordinary is divided into the two sections of the officials and of the soldiers, while the extraordinary is similarly divided into those of army and of battle affairs. As to the section of the samurai officials, they must wash their hands and feet night and morning and take a hot bath and so keep themselves clean. A samurai must do his hair every morning and keep the hair properly shaved from his forehead. Then he must always wear the ceremonial dress proper to the occasion and of course wear his two swords as well as carry a fan in his girdle. When he receives a guest he must treat him with the etiquette due to his rank and must refrain from idle talk. Even in taking a bowl of rice or a cup of tea it must be done correctly without slovenliness and with no lack of vigilance. If he is serving in some capacity when he is off duty he must not lounge about doing nothing but should read and practice writing, storing his mind with the ancient history and precepts of the warrrior houses and in short conducting himself at all times so that his manners are those proper to a samurai.

Next comes the section on soldiers. This concerns the exercise of fencing, spear practice, horsemanship, and shooting with bow and matchlock together with all else that pertains to the military art which must be enthusiastically studied and practiced so that all will be disciplined and resolute. And if these two codes of the samurai and the soldier are well understood, the ordinary ordinance may be considered complete, and this would appear to most people to be sufficient for the good warrior or official. But a samurai is an official for extraordinary conditions, and when the country is in a state of disorder he must lay aside the ordinary rule for samurai life and serve under his lord as commander, the greater and lesser retainers becoming officers and soldiers. Then all put away their dress of ceremony and don their armor and take arms in hand to advance into the enemy territory, and it is the various methods of arranging matters on such a campaign that are known as the rule of army affairs, and this is a thing that must be known. Then comes the rule of battle affairs, which is the method of handling the army when it comes into contact with the enemy to give battle. And if things go according to plan there is victory, and if not, there is defeat. This too is a thing the secrets of which must be understood. And what is called a first-class samurai is one who is skilled in all four sections of these two ordinances. To be experienced only in the two sections of the ordinary one may be sufficient for the duties of the average cavalier, but no one who is ignorant of the extraordinary sections can become a commander or high officer such as *monogashira* or *bugyō*. It is therefore most important that all samurai should consider and realize that they cannot rise to the highest positions without profound study of the extraordinary ordinance.

Never Neglect the Offensive Spirit

It is most important that one who is a samurai should never neglect the offensive spirit at any time and in all matters. For our country is different from other lands in that even the least of the people, farmers, merchants, and artisans, should all cherish some rusty blade, wherein is revealed the warrior spirit of this Empire of Nippon. These three classes are not, however, soldiers by profession, but it is the custom in the military families for even the very least of the servants of the samurai never to be without a short sword for a moment. Much more must the higher samurai always wear their girdle. And some very punctilious ones wear a blunt sword or a wooden one even when they go to the bath. And if this is so in the house how much more is it necessary when one leaves it to go somewhere else, since on the way you may well meet some drunkard or other fool who may suddenly start a quarrel. There is an old saying, "When you leave your gate, act as though an enemy was in sight." So since he is a samurai and wears a sword in his girdle he must never forget this spirit of the offensive. And when this is so the mind is firmly fixed on death. But the samurai who does not maintain this aggressive spirit, even though he does wear a sword at his side, is nothing but a farmer or a tradesman in a warrior's skin.

Recluse Samurai

From ancient times it has been the custom for samurai to become recluses, and indeed there is much resemblance between the two. For instance, among the Zen monks there are those called *zōsu* and *shuza* who are ordinary shavelings of the same standing as the outside retainers among the military class who are just ordinary soldiers of the companies. Then come the *tanryō* and *seidō*, a rank higher, who are more or less the equivalent of the *metsuke* (Censor) or Captains of the Guards or Captains of Infantry among the samurai. Then again among these same recluses there are some called *chōrō* or *oshō* who wear colored robes and carry a fly-whisk staff in their hand and have authority over the ordinary crowd just like the Commander of the Samurai or Commander of the Infantry, or again, the Six *Bugyō* of the Archers who are privileged to have their own standard and

surcoat and baton, and who issue orders to the army
and command in the field.

Only in the matter of learning these communities
of recluses seem to me to be far superior to those of
the samurai. And the reason is that it is the way of
the ordinary monks to leave their teachers and
travel around the country from one monastery to another for study and so to meet many distinguished
scholars and to accumulate merits in the practice
of meditation and virtue. And when they rise to be
tanryō and *seidō* and even *chōrō* and *oshō* and become
the abbots of great temples and monasteries, they
are still not in the least ashamed to continue their
study and research in order that they may be worthy
of promotion.

And so also I should like to see it among the samurai, but even ordinary samurai without office who do
outside service and have a good deal of time unoc-
cupied have quite a relatively good income and are
well provided with the necessities of life, so that
some who are still young have wives and children
and their only occupation seems to be a morning
and afternoon nap. They have not even studied the
two sections of the ordinary ordinance for samurai,
so much less have they any knowledge of the more
recondite extraordinary one, and so they go on
passing the months and years idly until their beards
grow white and their heads bald. Then, as they seem
to be about the age for it, they are assigned to the
status of those who are relieved of office, and if for

instance they should act as *tsukai-ban,* or envoy, they go off at once and get the assistance of some colleague and so carry it out, but should they be sent to some very distant province then they are flustered and distracted by the preparations for the journey, and when they do take up their duties they are barely able to carry them out by relying on instructions from seniors and borrowing books of reference, a state of things that cannot be considered the proper way. For as the duties of samurai are practically all fixed, they should consider them when they have nothing to do, and when they meet officers of capacity and experience they should cease idle talk and make a point of enquiring from them about matters on which they anticipate they will need advice. They must make themselves acquainted with all the facts and collect and copy old books and plans so that they are well informed about their duty at all points and then whatever they are ordered to do at any time they will find it easy to undertake. And if you depend on your seniors and colleagues for information and perform duties with their help, this may do for ordinary ones, but in the rare case when something unusual happens you may not be able to get any assistance and then for good or evil you must depend on your own ability to solve the problem. And an Inspector of the Forces has to know all about such things as the numbers of an enemy, the best place to make a camp and dispose the troops, the strength of castles, the advantages or disadvantages of geogra-

phical position and the probability of victory, so
that from ancient times this office has been regarded
as a difficult one. However, if an Inspector should
make a miscalculation in his views the matter will
most likely end only in blame for him, whereas those
above the rank of Infantry Commander *(ashigaru
taishō)*, who wield the marshal's baton and have the
actual control of the troops, are responsible for the
lives of all the men in their army. Therefore it is a
most reprehensible thing that men should disgrace
these high commands by swaggering in them without
any proper knowledge or capacity.

It is as though among the Zen monks one who
neglected his studies when he was a junior should,
merely by virtue of a bald head and superannuation,
be advanced to the rank of *chōrō* or *oshō*, wear gor-
geous robes and carry the fly-whisk and hold authority over multitudes of his brethren. Only should
an unworthy monk of this type be exalted to such
high preferment in an improper way, he would find
himself the laughing-stock of the whole community,
and be put to public shame and have to resign, so
that he would do no special harm to the order. But it
is very different with samurai who are promoted to
similar high office and are incompetent to command,
for they jeopardize the lives of all under them, and
the loss they can cause is very great. Therefore, they
must be very diligent to study whenever they have
any spare time so as to gain a thorough knowledge
of the ordinances of the army and of battle, for both

study and practice are most necessary to one who holds a high command.

Right and Wrong

One who is a warrior should have a thorough understanding of these two qualities. If he knows how to do the one and avoid the other then he will have attained to Bushido. And right and wrong are nothing but good and evil, for though I would not deny that there is a slight difference between the terms, yet to act rightly and do good is difficult and is regarded as tiresome, whereas to act wrongly and do evil is easy and amusing, so that naturally most incline to the wrong or evil and tend to dislike the right and good. But to be thus unstable and make no distinction between right and wrong is contrary to reason, so that anyone who understands this distinction and yet does what is wrong is no proper samurai, but a raw and untaught person. And the cause of it is small capacity for self-control. Though this may not sound so bad, if we examine into its origin we find it arises from cowardice. That is why I maintain that it is essential for a samurai to refrain from wrong and cleave to what is right.

Now in the matter of doing right there are three degrees. For instance, if a man goes on a journey with a neighbor and his companion has a hundred *ryo* of gold which, in order to avoid the trouble of carrying it with him, he deposits with this man till he comes back. And he does so without telling anyone about it. Then on the journey this neighbor is taken with a sudden illness from over-eating, or apoplexy, or something of the sort, and dies of it, so that there is nobody at all who knows anything about the money. But the other, out of pure sympathy and compassion and nothing else, and without a single evil thought, immediately informs the relatives and returns all the money to them. This is truly a man who does what is right. In the second case, suppose the man who had the money to have been one who had only a few acquaintances and was not intimate with anybody, so that no one would know about the money he had deposited and there would be none likely therefore to make enquiries. And if the other was not very well off he might well regard it as a lucky windfall and think it no harm to say nothing and keep it for himself. But then a sudden shame would come over him for having harbored such a polluting idea and he would put it from him at once and return the money. This is doing right on account of shame that proceeds from one's mind. Then there is the case where somebody in his house, either one of his family or of his servants, knows about this money, and he is ashamed of what that person may think or what may be said of him in the future and so returns it. This is one who does right from shame connected with other people. But here we may wonder what he would do if nobody knew anything about it. Still, we can hardly pronounce him to be a person who, though he does not know what is right, does it.

However, generally speaking, the rule for the practice of right conduct is that first of all we should feel shame at the contempt of our family and servants and friends, and then at the scorn of the wider circle of our acquaintances and of outsiders, and thus eschew the wrong and do right. This will then naturally become a habit and in time we shall acquire the disposition to prefer the right and dislike the wrong.

Again in the way of valor, he who is born brave will think it nothing to go into battle and come under a hot fire of arrows and bullets. Devoted to loyalty and duty he will make his body a target and press on, presenting by his splendid valor an indescribably fine example to all beholders. But on the other hand, there may be one whose knees tremble and whose heart palpitates as he wonders how he is going to manage to acquit himself decently in all this danger, but he goes on because he is ashamed to be the only one to falter under the eyes of his comrades as they advance, and because he fears loss of reputation in the future. So he hardens his resolution and presses on in no way behind the naturally valiant one. Thus, though he may be vastly inferior to the born brave, after several of these experiences he becomes used to it and finds his feet, and so eventually his courage is confirmed and he grows into a warrior by no means inferior to the born fearless. So both in doing right and in producing valor there is no other way but a sense of shame. For if people say of wrong that it does not matter and do it, and merely laugh if they see a coward and say that it does not matter either, what means will there be of disciplining this kind of person?

Bravery

For Bushido the three qualities of Loyalty, Right Conduct, and Bravery are essential. We speak of the loyal warrior, the righteous warrior, and the valiant warrior, and it is he who is endowed with all these three virtues who is a warrior of the highest class. But among the myriads of samurai it is rare to find one of this kind. Now the loyal warrior and the righteous one may not be difficult to be distinguished by their ordinary, everyday conduct, but it may be doubted whether in times of peace and quiet like the present it will be so easy to single out the brave one. This, however, is not so, for bravery does not show itself

first when a man puts on armor and takes spear
and halberd in hand and goes out to battle. You can
see whether he has it or not when he is sitting on the
mats leading his ordinary life. For he who is born
brave will be loyal and filial to his lord and parents,
and whenever he has any leisure he will use it for
study, neither will he be negligent in practicing
the military arts. He will be strictly on his guard
against indolence and will be very careful how he
spends every penny. If you think this shows detest-
able stinginess you will be mistaken, since he spends
freely where it is necessary. He does not do anything
that is contrary to the ordinances of his lord or that
is disliked by his parents, however much he may
wish. And so, ever obedient to his lord and his
parents, he preserves his life in the hope some day of
doing a deed of outstanding merit, moderating his
appetite for eating and drinking and avoiding over-
indulgence in sex, which is the greatest delusion of
mankind, so that he may preserve his body in health
and strength. For in these, as in all other things, it
is rigid self-control that is the beginning of valor.

But he who is not brave, on the other hand, will
appear to be only superficially loyal and filial to his
lord and parents and without any sincere intention
of remaining so. Indifferent to his lord's rules and
his parents' dislikes he is given to wanton strolling
where he should not be, doing what ought not to be
done, and in everything putting his own inclination
first. He loves to sleep both in the morning and

afternoon and particularly dislikes having to study. As for the military arts, he knows all about them but disdains to practice them, merely boasting about his skill at what he cannot do and full of enthusiasm about some useless folly. He spends any amount of money on luxurious feasting, and throws away his allowance and mortgages his salary without the least foresight. But where he ought to spend he is stingy and will not even bother to repair the chipped lacquer and broken cordage of the old armor he inherits from his father. Much less will he buy any new suits or any horse furniture to make up for losses. His health is too poor for him to serve his lord properly, and he has no consideration for the trouble and anxiety this causes his parents. He eats and drinks too much and is excessive in sex matters, and this using up and filing away of his physical powers and longevity is due to nothing but a weak and untutored mind incapable of self-control, and so we shall not be far wrong in diagnosing it as the source of cowardice in a samurai. And so can the valiant be distinguished from the pusillanimous, even while sitting on the mats at home.

Respect

The two Ways of Loyalty and Filial Duty are not limited to the samurai. They are equally incumbent on the Farmer, Artisan, and Merchant classes. But among these classes, for example, a child or servant while sitting with his parent or master may have his legs crossed or his hands anyhow, or he may speak to them standing while they are sitting, or may do various other unceremonious and impolite things and it does not matter. If he is really sincere in his filial feelings and truly cherishes his master or parent, that is all that is expected in the case of these three classes. But in Bushido, however loyal and filial a man may be in his heart, if he is lacking in the correct etiquette and manners by which respect is shown to lord or parent, he cannot be regarded as living in proper conformity with it. Any negligence of this kind not only towards his lord but also towards his parents is no conduct for anyone who sets up to be a samurai. And even when out of their sight and in private, there must be no relaxation and no light and shade in the loyalty and filial duty of a warrior. Wherever he may be lying down or sleeping, his feet must never for an instant be pointing in the direction of his lord's presence. If he sets up a straw bale for archery practice anywhere, the arrows must never fall toward the place where his lord is. Similarly, when he puts down his spear or halberd their points must never be in that direction either. And should he hear any talk about his lord, or should anything about him escape his own lips, if he is lying down he must spring up, and if he is sitting at ease he must straighten himself up, for that is the Way of the Samurai.

Other things that show a stupid lack of consideration are pointing the elbow toward where you know the lord is, talking about him while sprawling on the mats, throwing aside or tearing a letter by one's parents or using part of it to clean a pipe or night-light. People of such mentality are quite likely, when they meet outsiders, to speak ill of their lord's affairs. And if anyone, even a complete outsider, comes and talks adroitly to them, they will be quite pleased and unhesitatingly pour out a lot of scandal about their parents or elder brothers and speak ill of them and revile them. No doubt they will meet with punishment from their lord or with some other misfortune sometime or other and their end will not be one befitting a warrior; but even if they continue to live, it will be a worthless existence, certainly not a normal one of peace and prosperity. In former days, in the Keichō era, there lived a valiant warrior named Kani Saizō, a Commander of Infantry under

Fukushima Saemon-taiyu Masanori, who kept watch and ward day and night by the iron gate of the castle of Hiroshima in Aki. As he was an old man he would drop off to sleep in the intervals of duty, and it happened that a page of Masanori came to him and brought a young hawk with a message that it was a present from his master on one of these occasions. Saizō at once sprang up, put on the *hakama* that he had taken off and laid aside, turned toward the Hommaru and received it, saying that he would immediately call there to return thanks. Then he went on, "As for you, if you were my son I should call you a silly fool, for if you bring a message from our lord it is your business to say so at the beginning, so that I could be prepared for it, and not to give it to me when I am having a nap like this without any warning. It is a good thing you are not my son, and as you are only a page, I suppose you know no better and I must excuse you." The boy hurried away in dismay at this scolding and told his youthful comrades all about it, so that after a while it came to the ears of Masanori himself. So he called the page and questioned him about it, and when he confirmed the story his master said, "Saizō was quite right in being angry at such clumsiness. I wish all the samurai of Aki and Bizen had his spirit, for then there would be nothing they could not do."

Horsemanship

In ancient times, all samurai, high and low, considered archery and horsemanship as the first of the military arts, but more recently they prefer to practice with the sword and spear and then to value skill in riding. Moreover, it is very proper that the youthful samurai should continue to exercise daily in shooting with the bow and matchlock, in drawing the sword, and in *jujitsu* beside other martial arts, since when they grow older they will not have the time to practice what they wish.

So I would wish to see the young samurai pay particular attention to horsemanship and especially to get used to riding those horses that have faults and do not like to be ridden. For good horses and those easy to ride are comparatively rare since they are acquired by those of high rank and not likely to be found in the stables of the smaller fry. But if a man is a fine horseman and sees a mount that is quite a good one but has some defect, or bad habit, or likes to get rid of its rider, he can get it for a very reasonable price and so with his horse allowance he can be mounted considerably above his station. Points like the color or quality of a horse's coat can only affect those of high rank, and the small retainer cannot afford to despise an animal because he does not like its color or because its hair is poor, but if it is a good one he had better buy it and keep it.

Long ago in the province of Shinano there lived a certain Kakuganji of the Murakami house who was captain of a band of three hundred horsemen, good archers all of them. And he made it a family custom to select the horses he kept from those that others rejected for some defect in their appearance. He did not bother his men with exercise on the racecourse but took them out by fifty or a hundred into the rough ground around the castle town where was plenty of space and put himself at their head and galloped them about in all directions up and down and across country. And they would jump into the saddle and down again while their horses were going hard just as they chose, and rode so well that they made a great name for themselves. And even Takeda of Kai learnt to regard these men of Shinano as foes not to be defied with impunity, a very great tribute to Kakuganji's training.

Now the horse a warrior needs for war is one about one to three inches above middle height, with a middling head and stern according to tradition, but for a small retainer with no spare mount it is better that his one horse should be a decidedly tall one, and he should not mind its head being high while he should rejoice at the width of its stern, the kind that is called a six-foot rump. But to like such unnatural and deforming tricks as stretching the sinews of the legs to give a longer stride or cutting those of the tail to prevent its being raised is to show a craving for oddity quite inconsistent with Bushido. For a horse with the sinews of its legs unnaturally stretched soon gets tired and is useless for a long journey uphill or for crossing rivers. And one with its tail sinews cut is apt to slip his crupper when jumping over a ditch or canal. But a too broad rump is said not to be good for negotiating a narrow path.

Now there are two ways for a warrior to regard horses, a good and a bad. The ancient warrior regarded his horse as an indispensable means of carrying him when he was clad in heavy armor with banner and war-gear complete, which he could never have sustained on his two feet alone. And as it might happen that the horse might be wounded or even killed, though it was but an animal he felt a great compassion for it and took great care of it and saw that it was always well fed. But what people think of now is to buy a faulty mount at a low price and correct his defects, or to know how to pick out a country-bred colt and train him, so that they can sell to somebody who takes a fancy to him at a good profit. This is the mentality of a vet or a horse coper and a very poor standard for a connoisseur.

The Military Arts

One who is a samurai, even though but a small retainer, certainly ought to provide himself with a suitable instructor and study the traditional military arts so that he knows all there is to be known on the subject. Some may say that it is not at all necessary for a small samurai, but this I consider a very shallow view, since in all ages there have been a number of warriors who have risen from quite humble positions to make a name as great generals and to become lords of districts and provinces. And even now I do not think it impossible for a small vassal to become a commander of an army. Moreover, study of the military arts will make one who is naturally clever more so and one who is born somewhat dull rather less so. Therefore, all samurai ought certainly to apply themselves to it. But a bad use can be made of this study to puff oneself up and disparage one's colleagues by a lot of high-flown but incorrect arguments that only mislead the young and spoil their spirit. For this kind gives forth a wordy discourse that may appear to be correct and proper enough, but actually he is only striving for effect and thinking of his own advantage, so the result is the deterioration of his character and the loss of the real samurai spirit. This is a fault arising from a superficial study of the subject, so those who begin it should never be satisfied to go only halfway but persevere until they understand all its secrets and only then return to their former simplicity and live a quiet life. But if people spend a lot of time in this study and only get halfway and are quite unable to master it, they may not be able to regain their former simple condition, but lapse into a confused state that is most unfortunate. And by their former simplicity or ignorance I mean their mentality before they began to study the military arts. There is an old saying that bean sauce that smells of bean sauce is no good and so it is with the military pedants.

CHAPTER II

Household Management

One who is a samurai should, if he finds in his wife
matters that do not please him, admonish her to
agree with him by reasonable argument, though in
trifles it is well that he be indulgent and patient
with her. But if her disposition is consistently bad
and he considers she will be of no further use, he may
divorce her and send her home to her parents under
exceptional circumstances. But should he not do
this but keep her as his wife so that people address
her by the respectful titles of *okusama* and *kamisama*,
and then shout at her and revile her with all sorts of
abusive expressions, he is behaving in a way that
may be suitable to hirelings and coolies who live in
the back streets of the business quarter but is certainly not proper for a samurai who is a cavalier.
Much less is it fitting for such a one to lay his hand
on his sword or menace his wife with his clenched
fist, an outrageous thing that only a cowardly

samurai would think of doing. For a girl born in a warrior house and of age to be married would never, if she were a man, for a moment tolerate being threatened by the fist of anyone. It is only because she is unfortunately born a woman that she has to shed tears and put up with it. And to act in a bullying manner to one who is weaker than himself is a thing that a brave samurai never does. And he who likes and does what a brave man hates and avoids is rightly described as a coward.

Relatives

Usually among farmers and tradesmen the children of both elder and younger brothers are styled nephews, as are those of married sisters, and are treated in the same way, but among samurai it is different. For instance, the son of an elder brother who is the heir, though he is a nephew, since he will carry on the elder brother's house and so is the heir-presumptive, is respected as an elder brother and treated with deference accordingly. This is not the ordinary treatment of a nephew but is because he represents the ancestral founder of the family. As to the second and third sons, it is sufficient if the ordinary relations of uncle and nephew be maintained as with the sons of younger brothers. Sisters' children are nephews also, but as they have outside affinities this should be kept in mind, and it is well to use ordinary communications with them, both spoken and written, and keep them at a distance. Nephews and younger brothers and one's own children too, if they are sent out as adopted children, must of course be treated as such. Whether one meets them in private or exchanges words with them at some family meeting, greetings and salutations should be of a formal and distant nature as with those of outside houses and families and distinct from those of near relations. For if after they have gone to another house you treat them as son or younger brother still, it will look as though you would rather have kept them at home and that attitude will be regarded as a slight by the adoptive father and the other family. Only this adoptive father is certainly not a relative, and supposing there should be disorder in his house and the succession appears to be difficult, then it may be quite proper to treat a son or younger brother as such and to help them and not to forsake them.

Again, when you marry your daughter into another family, and a son is born to her and the husband dies so that the small grandson is left as the heir, in the matter of the arrangement of the estate when you have to enter into negotiations with the relations and connections of this son-in-law, it is essential that, out of ten points for instance, you leave eight or nine to be decided by them. And even when the husband is alive, if the family is badly off and becomes a burden on the relatives, since one can hardly refrain from doing something to assist one's daughter when in difficulties, it is proper to give some help.

Thrift

Samurai who are in service, both great and small, must always practice thrift and have the discrimination to do it so that they do not have a deficit in their household expenditure. As to those with a large income, if they do find they are living beyond their means they can quickly make a change in their affairs, and by taking care and making a saving here and cutting down something there, they can soon recover their solvency because they have a certain surplus. But if a small retainer tries to live like a great vassal and so incurs unnecessary expense and gets into difficulties, he cannot recover himself because he has nothing to fall back on, and however much he tries to economize, he only becomes more involved until at last he comes to complete ruin. And as people's domestic affairs are a private matter, and one who is in service has to do as his colleagues do and must incur certain necessary expenses, he will be driven to every possible trick and device, even to saying what should not be said and doing what should not be done, for it is financial difficulty that induces even those with a high reputation to do dishonest things that are quite alien to them. So that one must make a firm resolve to live only according to one's means and be very careful not to indulge in any useless expenses, spending money only on what is necessary, for this is what is called the Way of Economy. But about this there is one thing that must be noted. To do nothing but talk about economy and hate to spend anything, saving and skimming everywhere, and being delighted when you can add one coin to another by some tightfisted trick, is to acquire a mentality devoted to filthy lucre and eventually lose all sense of decency so as to do what ought not to be done and leave undone what should be done. People of this type lose all instincts except that of hoarding and what they practice is miserliness and not economy. However it may be with peasants and merchants, stinginess in a samurai is as much to be abhorred as throwing away the Three Sacred Treasures. For if he puts all the money there is before duty and grudges to spend it, how much more will he grudge throwing away his much more precious life. That is why those of old said that in China parsimony is regarded as synonymous with cowardice.

House Construction

For a samurai who is in service it is quite fitting that he should have his outer gate and guardhouse, his porch and entrance as well as his reception room, as fine as may be consistent with his income. For in all castle towns people from elsewhere come in as far as the outer moats to look around, and if the residences of the samurai are of good appearance without and quiet and dignified within, it will rebound to the credit of their lord as well as of themselves. But otherwise the inner parts of the house where the wife and family live should be considered adequate however unsightly they may be, provided they keep out the rain, for it is most important that one should spend as little as possible on repairs or renovations. For in this unsettled world even the lord of a castle has always to keep in mind the possibility of a siege, and the samurai residences within the second and third wards must be kept low and of little depth and inexpensive to build. Much more then must those retainers, who live in the outer ward, who may have to burn and obliterate their houses in time of emergency, refrain from building anything very permanent. It should in fact be of the lightest possible construction and no more than a shed to sleep in. Realizing all this, even in this present peaceful age, a samurai who wishes to keep his Bushido unsullied will certainly not think of his house as a permanent residence or lavish any care on any elaborate decoration. Besides, when it catches fire one has to put up a suitable shelter again in a hurry, so that anyone who does not anticipate this but spends too much money on building, and even perhaps runs into debt for it with pleasure, can only be considered quite lacking in a sense of the fitness of things.

Weapons

Every samurai who is in service must have a supply of weapons suitable to his means. Every feudal house has its military regulations, and the proper banners and flags and helmet insignia, spear mounts, sleeve crests, and marks on the baggage animals as ordered by the lord must be carefully provided in a uniform manner. For if they have to be improvised in a hurry it will be an obvious sign of carelessness and will provoke contempt. Men who from neglect of these insignia have been attacked by their own side and killed and suffered loss are not unknown in military history, so there must be no want of precaution in these things. And some may think that their servants are not likely to have to cut anybody down and so may replace the blades of their swords with wood or bamboo, and neglect to provide them with a loincloth because they think they will not need to gird up their clothes, and find themselves in difficulties owing to their want of foresight. And a samurai who is a cavalier and who receives a considerable stipend and who does not know when he may have to take the field, however peaceful the time may appear to be, is a hundred percent more culpable if he does not provide himself with the proper weapons than the young serving man with a wooden sword or no loincloth. So from fear of being put to public shame he ought to equip himself properly. And here is a piece of advice on the subject. When a small retainer wishes to fit himself out with armor and has, let us say, three pieces of gold to get a suit, the best thing he can do will be to spend two-thirds of it on the body armor and helmet, leaving the remainder to provide all the other things he will need such as underclothes, breeches, coat, under-*hakama*, upper girdle, surcoat, whip, fan, wallet, cloak, water-bottle, cup, etc., so that he will have every accessory he needs as well as his suit of armor. Then, though he may be young and very strong, it is better to avoid heavy suits of thick iron armor and weighty banners and standards, for the very good reason that, though they may be tolerable while he is young and vigorous, as he grows older they will become too much for him. And even a young man may fall ill or be wounded, and then the lightest iron armor will be a heavy burden and a hindrance. And if a young man gets known for the weight of his banners and standards he will find it difficult to give them up when he becomes older and less able to support them.

On the Equipment of Servants

A small retainer, even on extraordinary occasions, should not go about with many servants and so need not have more than one spear. And should that one get damaged he will be without a spear to be carried before him. So he should keep a spear-blade and this can be fitted with a bamboo shaft so that it can be used in the meantime, for it is important that something should be provided for the present. And if it is only slightly damaged you can provide a rather long, strongly mounted sword and let the attendants carry that. The young squires may use a *dōmaru* armor with an iron helmet, and the underservants and attendants a *munekake* with a towel around their head or an iron hat, for a small retainer should be careful to arm his men lightly. And if you have a bout at fencing, and armor and helmet are used, your sword will probably get its edge turned and you will need to replace it with another. Then the old one can be used by the young squire and is again given to the sandal-bearer or ostler.

Samurai

Since samurai are officials whose business it is to destroy rebels and disorderly elements and give peace and security to the three classes of the people, even the least of those who bear this title must never commit any violence or injustice against these three classes. That is to say, he must not demand any more revenue than is customary from the farmers or wear them out by forced service. He must not order articles from artisans and then neglect to pay them, neither must he send for things from townspeople and tradesmen and keep them waiting for their money, while it is most incorrect to lend them money and take usury on it as a mere sleeping partner. One should always be considerate to these people, sympathetic to the farmers on one's estates and careful that artisans are not ruined. And though you may not at once settle the debts you may have incurred in transactions with townspeople and tradesmen, you certainly ought to pay something off them from time to time so as not to cause these classes loss and distress. Samurai whose duty it is to chastize robbers and thieves must not imitate the ways of these criminals.

Sense of Shame

Fifty or sixty years ago, in speaking of employment, lordless samurai would say that a man was hardly able to keep a spare horse, when they meant an income of something over five hundred *koku,* or that one could just afford to keep a half-starved beast if he had about three hundred. Similarly, if there was a question of getting a position with an income of a hundred, they would describe it as allowing a man to have one rusty spear. For up until then the ancient style of the samurai still survived and it was not their way to mention figures and say that anyone had so many *koku* of income, so they used these expressions. "A hawk may be starving but he won't touch corn," and, "The samurai may have eaten nothing but he uses his toothpick," are sayings that illustrate this sentiment. Young people then never spoke of profit or loss or mentioned the price of anything and would blush if they heard any talk of love affairs. And though they may not be able to reach them, I think all samurai ought to admire and study these ancient ideals. "Though a man's nose be crooked, if he can breathe through it, all is well," is the way we should regard it.

Choice of Friends

For a samurai who is in service it is most important that he associates with and makes friends of only those among his colleagues who are valiant, dutiful, wise and influential. But as men of this kind are not very numerous, he may find only one among his various friends on whom he can thoroughly rely in time of need. Generally speaking, it is not desirable for a samurai to make any intimate friend of whom he is specially fond and with whom he prefers to eat and drink and go about. For if he discovers a kindred spirit and makes a great friend of him, thinking he will be an amusing boon companion, they may easily come to behave in a manner quite unsuitable to their class, treating each other without any ceremony, sprawling up against each other, spending their evenings bawling songs and *joruri* ballads, using too familiar terms of address and apparently most intimate one moment, and then, from insistence on some trifle, falling out and not on speaking terms the next. Then they may as quickly make it up without even employing the good offices of a reconciler as is usual. Such contemptible want of dignity shows that though outwardly some may look like samurai their minds are those of day laborers.

Friendship

Reliability is one of the qualities of the Way of the Warrior required of a samurai, but it is by no means desirable that he should proffer assistance without any special reason, put himself forward in things that do not matter, or take on himself obligations in affairs that do not concern him, just for the sake of doing so or of giving his advice. Even in things that do concern him to a slight extent it is much better to hold aloof, if no one asks him to interfere.

Because even small questions, let alone more complicated ones, if a samurai becomes implicated in them, may involve him so that he cannot withdraw without risking his precious life which should be at the disposal only of his lord or his parents. Therefore, I say that he should not be needlessly obliging.

If the samurai of former days was asked a favor he would consider whether it was one that could be granted or not, and if the latter, he would decline at once. And if he did entertain it, he would only undertake it after further careful thought, so that he was quite prepared to deal with it and the whole affair was soon settled. In consequence the suppliant's difficulties were resolved and the benefactor gained great praise. If, on the contrary, without this reflection anyone takes on himself some responsibility, he will be unable to carry it through properly and gain a reputation for being unprincipled when this becomes apparent. Then again, giving one's advice or opinion should only be done after mature consideration. For though parents, teachers, elder brothers, uncles, and so on may give unsuitable advice to their children, pupils, and nephews without much harm, everything that comes out of the mouth of a samurai must be considered and guarded. And particularly to his friends and colleagues must he be most judicious in his utterances. And when he is singled out and asked to take part in a consultation he may of course say that he has no views on the subject and refuse to discuss it. But if he does become a party to the discussion, he will be most helpful, if he states exactly what he thinks, clearly and succinctly without reserve and without any regard for the disapproval or resentment the others may show. For if, out of weakness, for fear of opposing people or offending them, he exhibits a maladroit hesitancy, and turns aside from what is just and agrees with what is not reasonable, and, in order to avoid a rupture, allows unsuitable things to be said and burdens to be laid on others, then he will eventually be voted a futile councillor and reviled and despised into the bargain. Again, if anyone is so stupid as to think himself too much of a personage to take part in a confabulation, arguing that there is no need of consultation but wishing to decide everything according to his own opinion, and so making a mess of things, he is likely to find himself not very popular among his fellows as the result.

Breaking Off Relations

A samurai who is in service may well have among his acquaintances or comrades one with whom for some reason he does not wish to associate. But if he is ordered by his lord to serve with such a one he should immediately go to him and say, "I am ordered to serve with you, and though so far we have not been on speaking terms, as things are, I trust you will cooperate with me so that we can carry out our duties properly without any difficulties." And should the other be his senior in office, he will ask him to give him the benefit of his kind instruction. If the day after he should be transferred to some other position, then they are to revert to their former terms, but that meanwhile they are to agree to work together cordially in their official duties is the correct conduct for a samurai. How much more between comrades who have no such impediment should there always be the most hearty mutual cooperation when they are serving together. But those who are always striving for power, and when others are new to office and all unacquainted with its details, lack the kindness of heart to give them assistance and help them to function efficiently, and even rejoice when they make mistakes, these show a nasty mean spirit and are entirely worthy of censure. This is the sort of samurai who will do some dirty trick like turning against his own side when he finds himself in an awkward situation, so anything of the kind is to be strictly avoided.

Reputations

One who is a samurai should continually read the ancient records so that he may strengthen his character. For those works that are famous everywhere, such as the *Kōyō Gunkan,* the *Nobunagaki,* and the *Taikōki,* give accounts of battles with detailed descriptions and the names of those who did gallant deeds as well as the numbers of those who fell. And among these latter the great vassals ought presumedly to have figured considerably, but actually they were not so conspicuous for their valor and so their names are not recorded. Even among the small retainers only those whose martial valor was preeminent have been selected, and their names inscribed for posterity. And both the fallen who have left no name behind and those whose exploits are famous through the ages felt only the same pain when their heads were cut off by the enemy. So consider this well. As he has to die, the aim of a samurai should be to fall performing some great deed of valor that will astonish both friend and foe alike and make his death regretted by his lord and commander and so leave behind a great name to the generations to come. Very different is the fate of the coward who is the last to charge and the first to retire, and who, in an attack on a stronghold, uses his comrades as a shield against the enemy missiles. Struck by a chance arrow he falls and dies a dog's death, and may even be trampled underfoot by his own side. This is the greatest disgrace for a samurai, and should never be forgotten but pondered over earnestly day and night.

Braggarts and Slanderers

These two types may seem to be very much alike but in fact they are very different. In former days there were very many who had the reputation for being braggarts among the samurai, for example Matsudaira Kagaemon and Ōkubo Hikozaemon, both officers of the shogun's guard. In fact, in those days every daimyo was likely to have several samurai who were of this type. They were men with many great exploits to their credit and in no way deficient in the Way of the Warrior, but on occasions apt to be obstinate and so difficult parties in a conference. And when they were pressed in their living conditions and some incident arose from their income and office being incompatible with their high reputation, they would become reckless and say what they pleased without any regard for their company. But their lord and the councillors and elders of their clan would overlook it and take no notice, so that they became more and more willful and would tell anyone what they thought of their good or bad points without reserve or apology, and so they continued to do all their days. Such were the braggarts of old, men with a record of great deeds. But the braggarts of today are fellows who have never even put on a suit of mail, and who spend most of their time sitting with their friends and acquaintances discussing the defects of their lord's government, and pointing out the failings of the councillors and commissioners, and certainly not omitting the misdeeds of their own comrades, while at the same time emphasizing their own superiority. Such shallow pates are a world apart from the brave braggarts of old, and should properly be styled slanderers or claptrap fools.

Travel

A samurai in service when on a journey, if he is a small retainer, should ride with the baggage on a packhorse. And in case he falls off he should tie up his two swords together so that they do not slip from their scabbards. But to tie up the hilt of the long sword into a thick bundle with a three-foot towel is a thing that ought not to be done. The same can be said of tying up the sheath of the spear with a thick rope to keep it on. There must not be the least carelessness about these things. And if you put on your baggage insignia or labels, "Retainer of Lord So-and-so," it may appear somewhat disrespectful to his house. And when, as is the custom on journeys nowadays, you get a horse direct from the ostler, if the previous rider is a samurai, you should wait to dismount yourself until he has dismounted at the bidding of the ostler. And the reason is that if you dismount at the bidding of the groom and stand there, the other will be constrained to change his mount though it may be he had not that intention. And if one has taken the trouble to get off a horse, he may feel embarrassment if he has to mount again.

In crossing rivers en route one should always engage a wading coolie, for if you grudge the expense or think you are an expert in the water, and cross without one and your horse falls and the luggage gets wet and perhaps a servant is injured, you will look very foolish.

Or again, with the idea of shortening the journey, if you ride at Yokkaichi or get on a boat at Awazu, you will be very shortsighted. For if you go by the ordinary boat from Kuwana and then meet with rough weather you have some excuse, but if you take a lot of trouble and go by a by road and there is any mishap, there is none at all. So the old verse advises,

> Does the warrior think
> That the ford at Yabase
> Is the nearer way?
> He should know the shortest road
> Goes round by the Seta Bridge.

And this principle of the longest way being the shortest does not only apply to roads. It must be kept in mind in everything.

Backbiting

A samurai who is in a lord's service must always be very careful not to indulge in underhand censure of any faults of his comrades that he may come to hear of or see. For a man cannot calculate how far he may not have unwittingly mistaken or misunderstood these things. Moreover, the clan officials and particularly the Councillors and Senior Officers are the spokesmen of the views of their lord, so that any criticism of them is a reflection on him. Then again, you may some day have to approach them with some request, and to consider their mood and clasp the hands and bend the knees and humbly entreat their favor, and suddenly to have to change your tone when just before you have been slandering anyone behind his back is the kind of thing no samurai ought to bring himself to do however weighty the business.

War Substitute

In the civil war period when battles were continuous, if a samurai was killed after a gallant fight or died of wounds received in it, his lord or commander would, out of regard for his services, allow his son, if he had one, however young, to inherit his position and emoluments. But if this son was only an infant he could not do any military service, so his father's younger brother, if he were not in service, would inherit the position of his elder brother and be appointed by his lord as his guardian. And he would then be known as a *jindai* or "War Substitute." And concerning this there is an ancient usage. For in such a case, though taking the position of elder brother, he should regard the child as his son, though actually his nephew, and should care for him and educate him as such. And as taking the place of the head of the house he should collect all the arms and armor and horse trappings and the other various possessions that belong to it, and with one or two other members of the family, should go over everything carefully and enter them all in a book.

Then when the child has grown up to the age of fifteen, so that the next year he will anyhow become an independent cavalier among the younger retainers, it is proper to put in a petition that he may be allowed to enter his lord's service and have his salary that he had been granted paid to him. And according to the quality of the person this petition may be granted, or again it is possible that on account of his youth the guardian may be requested to serve a few more years. But, however pressing this suggestion may be, he should definitely refuse it, and when the petition is granted, he should produce the inventory of the property that he made previously and hand over all the effects of the late father. And any goods that he may have acquired during the exercise of his guardianship that it seems proper to give should also be added to the list and handed over. Also, when he took over the headship of the house the War Substitute may have had assigned to him part of the income, for instance two hundred *koku* out of a total of five hundred, the remaining three hundred being left for the nephew. This may have been a piece of luck for him but quite the reverse for the main house, whose emoluments were thereby diminished, so he must request that his elder brother's original income be assigned to the heir in its entirety. Such is the proper conduct for a samurai who becomes a War Substitute. On the other hand, there is the one who is not willing to hand over to the heir when he comes of age, or when he does he leaves the property in bad condition and the house out of repair and makes no attempt to restore them. Worse still, he may bequeath to the heir debts that his father had not contracted, besides bothering the young man continually for rations and allowances and the like. Such a man is an unprincipled rascal.

The Latter End

The samurai, whether great or small, high or low, has to set before all other things the consideration of how to meet his inevitable end. However clever or capable he may have been, if he is upset and wanting in composure and so makes a poor showing when he comes to face it all, his previous good deeds will be like water and all decent people will despise him so that he will be covered with shame.

For when a samurai goes out to battle and does valiant and splendid exploits and makes a great name, it is only because he made up his mind to die. And if unfortunately he gets the worst of it and he and his head have to part company, when his opponent asks for his name he must declare it at once loudly and clearly and yield up his head with a smile on his lips and without the slightest sign of fear. Or should he be so badly wounded that no surgeon can do anything for him, if he is still conscious, the proper procedure for a samurai is to answer the enquiries of his superior officers and comrades and inform them of the manner of his being wounded and then to make an end without more ado.

Similarly in times of peace the steadfast samurai, particularly if he is old but no less if he is young and stricken with some serious disease, ought to show firmness and resolution and attach no importance to leaving this life. Naturally if he is in high office, but also however low his position may be, while he can speak he should request the presence of his official superior and inform him that as he has for long enjoyed his consideration and favor, he has consequently wished fervently to do all in his power to carry out his duties, but unfortunately he has now been attacked by this serious disease from which it is difficult to recover, and consequently is unable to do so; and that as he is about to pass away he wishes to express his gratitude for past kindness and trusts to be remembered respectfully to the Councillors of the clan. This done, he should say farewell to his family and friends and explain to them that it is not the business of a samurai to die of illness after being the recipient of the great favors of his lord for so many years, but unfortunately in his case it is unavoidable. But they who are young must carry on his loyal intentions and firmly resolve to do their duty to their lord, ever increasing this loyalty so as to serve with all the vigor they possess. Should they fail to do this or act in any disloyal or undutiful way, then even from the shadow of the grass his spirit will disown and disinherit them. Such is the leave-taking of a true samurai.

And in the words of the Sage too it is written that when a man is about to die his words should be such as appear right. This is what the end of a samurai should be, and how different is it from that of one who refuses to regard his complaint as incurable and is worried about dying, who rejoices if people tell him he looks better and dislikes it if they say he looks worse, the while he fusses with doctors and gets a lot of useless prayers and services said for him and is in a complete state of flurry and confusion. As he gradually gets worse he does not say anything to anyone but ends by bungling the one death he has so that it is no better than that of a dog or cat. This is because he does not keep death always before his eyes as I recommended him to do in my first chapter, but puts any mention of it away from him as ill-omened and seems to think he will live forever, hanging on to existence with a greedy intensity. One who goes into battle in this cowardly spirit is not likely to die a glorious death in a halo of loyalty, so one who values the samurai ideal should see that he knows how to die properly of illness on the mats.

CHAPTER III

Service

When a samurai is in service it may well happen
that his lord has very large expenses to meet and his
circumstances become straitened in consequence,
so that he has to borrow part of the salaries of his
retainers for a certain number of years. And in this
case, whether the amount is great or small, it is
highly improper for a samurai to suggest, or even
hint in the privacy of his family, much less outside it,
that this causes him any difficulty or embarrassment.
For from of old it has been the custom for retainers to
rally to the help of their lord in his time of need
just as he has always been ready to help them in
theirs. And when a lord is pressed by private liabil-
ities so that it affects his public duties and prevents
him from undertaking things it is considered the
business of a daimyo to do, and has to put up with
a lot of annoyance as a result, this must be a very
painful thing for his retainers to contemplate.

77

However, ordinary affairs can go on somehow, but suppose there should happen tomorrow some unexpected disturbance on the frontier of the province and our contingent be ordered to start at once to take up some position, the first thing that would be needed would be money. But however clever one may be, this commodity cannot be produced immediately; as the proverb has it, like a man with his hand caught under a stone who cannot move in any direction, it would be difficult to do anything, and yet the other daimyos will all be ready to start on the fixed day, and that day cannot be altered, so that all unprepared as we are there is no escape from setting out too.

In times of peace a military procession makes a brave show and people from the country come crowding into the houses of the towns to see it, so that it is exposed to the view of all classes, and if our array is inferior to the others it is a lifelong shame to the lord and his captains. So when we consider all this and its importance, all samurai, both great and small, old retainers and recently joined ones, must not fail to contribute a suitable proportion of their salary. And during this period of reduced income everyone has to use his brains a little and contrive to cut down the number of men and horses and wear garments of cotton and paper in winter and cotton *katabira* in summer. Then for the morning and evening meals only unpolished rice and rice bran and *misoshiru* must be eaten, and everyone must split his own wood and draw his own water and make his wife cook the rice and in fact put up with every possible hardship, for it is the duty of all who are in the service of a lord to bend all their energies to keep his affairs in proper order. And if we put up with these difficulties even in this period of economy, we can meet any special need of our lord and raise some emergency expenses. For one can, for instance, pawn his spare sword and his wife's workbox, and with the value of these he will have enough without borrowing. Even if your lord does not hear of it or the Councillors and Superior Officers despise you for it, it is an unspeakable thing that a samurai should be thought to make complaints about the reduction of his salary.

A Vassal's Duty

A samurai who is a cavalier and is favored with a salary by his lord must not call his life or his person his own. But among those who render military service there are two types. There are the petty retainers and *chugen,* or attendants, and so on who get no leisure either day or night but have to work hard all the time, but who are not necessarily bound to lay down their lives for their master and so cannot be considered culpable if they do not show themselves specially trained or skilled in martial exercises. For they are really only employees who sell their labor as workers and nothing else. But the bushi or samurai is quite different, for he is a servant who gives his life as well. His lord too is a similar vassal but on a different scale, for should any trouble arise in the empire he also has to render military service suitable to his status. That is to say, if he has a fief of 100,000 *koku* he has to provide 170 horsemen, 60 foot archers, 350 matchlock-men, 150 spearmen and 20 banners according to the statute of the shogun's government, while the number of his men beyond this is according to his inclination and the capacity of his commander. And beside this force that he has to lead out to war he must also have a sufficient number of men left behind in his castle town to protect it against attack. So that though he does not need them all the time he has to maintain a large number of samurai of all kinds. And among these there are a number who are incapable or who are born crippled or who seem wanting in spirit, but whose defects are magnanimously overlooked so that they can continue to draw their hereditary salaries. Therefore, what a retainer ought to bear in mind is how many are the retainers of all the lords of provinces and castles in the whole Empire of Japan who are thus bound to their masters by such mutual ties of affinity and who are receiving from them very considerable emoluments, in that for instance such a small salary as a hundred *koku* will in ten years amount to a thousand *koku,* and if it has been paid for several generations to the family for very many tens of years, what a very large sum will it not amount to? And in return for all this great favor the retainer does his ordinary peacetime duty as guard or company officer or inspector, a commonplace sort of performance that can scarcely be called outstanding service. But there may be at any time a sudden call to arms and then he may take his place in the ranks as a leading spearman, or, if it is an attack on a castle, as a vanguard horseman, or, if his side has a reverse, as a rear guard in the retreat, or, if his quality is equal to it, he may even take the place of his lord or commander and give his life for them under the arrowhail of the foe and die a splendid death where he stands without yielding an inch. Then indeed is the deepest sense of service in the samurai when he steels his resolution and shouts, "*Marishiten* be my witness, I will show you a deed that no other shall do!" And since to achieve this height of devotion he cannot call his body or soul his own, and he never knows when he may not have to render such service to his lord, he must take care not to damage his health by overeating or drinking or sex indulgence; neither must he regard death on the mats at home as his proper end. Much more must he be on his guard against disputes and quarrels with his comrades that may lead to blows, and risk the useless waste of lives in a disloyal and undutiful manner. To this end it is essential to think carefully before you speak, for it is out of words that disputes arise. And when disputes grow hot, abuse is apt to follow, and when one samurai abuses another the affair can hardly end amicably. So if there is any risk of a dispute, remember that your life does not belong to you but to your lord, and so control your temper that the matter goes no further, for such is the duty of a discreet and loyal samurai.

The Duties of Samurai

The duties of samurai are twofold, military and constructive. When the land is at war he must be in the camp and the field day and night and can never know a moment's rest. And it is with the camp that construction is associated, for what with strongholds and moats and embattled camps and fortified outposts all ranks have to work continuously as fast and as strenuously as possible. But in peaceful times there is no camp duty and consequently none of the construction connected with it, so the various ranks of samurai under their commanders are allotted to fixed duties as guards, escorts, inspectors, and the like, and come to regard these stay-at-home functions as the normal ones for a warrior family, and think of field service as nothing but a dream of the past. Then, when at times the honor of assisting the shogun's government in its buildings is conferred on the daimyos and the expense of this is so great that they have to pass some of it onto their retainers, and request a contribution of a percentage of their salaries, they grudge it and grumble as though it were an exaction, because they do not realize that to take part in both military and constructive activities is the regular business of samurai. So you find some looking on their ordinary peacetime duties as quite a hardship and putting in an aegrotat even when there is nothing the matter with them, and heedless of the bother they cause others when they ask them to take their place. Then again, if they are sent out as Traveling Inspector they resent the fatigue of the journey and the expense incurred and put in an aegrotat for that also, and push off the trouble and expense onto their comrades without being in the least abashed at the contempt they earn. And even if the place to which they are sent is quite near, they complain openly about having to go out twice in one day or else about the unfavorable state of the weather. People who do their duty in this mean spirit, as though it were nothing but an imposition, are nothing but low-down grooms and servants in the skins of samurai.

The warriors who were born in the age of civil war were always in the field, scorched in their armor under the summer skies or pierced through its chinks by the winter blasts, soaked by the rain and cloaked by the snow, sleeping on moor and hill with no pillow but their mailed sleeve and with nothing to eat or drink but unhulled rice and salt soup. And whether they had to fight in the field or to attack a fortress or defend one they thought it no special hardship or trial but all in the ordinary day's work. When we reflect on this and how we, born in times of peace, can sleep under a mosquito net in summer and wrap ourselves in quilts in winter, and in fact live at ease eating what we fancy at any time of day, we should indeed consider ourselves lucky. But there is no reason why we should regard indoor guard duty or inspecting in the neighborhood as a serious burden. There was a certain Baba Mino, a veteran of renown under the house of Takeda of Kai, who wrote out and hung up on the wall as his life's maxim the four characters that signify "The field of battle is my normal abode."

Circumspection

Anyone who receives from his lord a present of a *kosode* or *kamishimo* with the lord's crest on it should be careful, when he wears the former, to put on a *kamishimo* with his own crest over it, or if it is the *kamishimo* with his lord's crest that he wears then he should don a *kosode* with his own. For if he wears a garment with the lord's crest only it might look as though he were a relative, and that would be impolite. And when these garments with the lord's crest become too old to be worn any longer the crests should be cut off them and burnt, so that they may not be soiled and treated with disrespect.

Again when any of your neighbors is either very ill or suffering from some bereavement, even though you may not be very intimate with him, you should take care not to indulge in any music or loud laughter, and give orders to your family and servants to do likewise. This is not only because of what they may think but to avoid the shame of being despised by neighbors and comrades as a mannerless boor.

Records

A samurai in service, even the latest joined retainer, much more the veteran, should be sure to make himself well versed in the history of his lord's family, its origin, its ancestral records and its connections, as well as in the accounts of the deeds of any of his comrades who are distinguished. And this he should do by enquiring about them from the senior members of the clan. For otherwise when he meets outsiders and in the course of conversation turns out to be ignorant of these matters, even if he is considered a good retainer in all other points, he will be held in little estimation.

Escort

When a samurai in service accompanies his lord on a journey and they arrive at a post-station it is most important that he should before sunset take care to make enquiries of the people of the locality, and note any hill or wood or shrine or temple and take his bearings by them, and find out in what direction from their lodging there is an open space and what is the condition of the road. This should be done so that should a fire suddenly break out during the night and it be necessary for his lord to retire he will be able to lead the way and know where to guide him. And when he accompanies his lord on foot, to remember to go in front of him on a hill and behind him on a slope may seem a small matter, but it is one a retainer should not overlook. For it is the duty of a samurai to be vigilant and careful at all times to think out how he can render any possible service in the calling to which he is appointed.

Officials

There is a saying that officials and white garments are best when new, and though but a joke I think it is true. For a white *kosode* looks very beautiful when new but after it has been worn for some time first the collar and sleeve edges get soiled and then it soon becomes a dirty rat color and is very unpleasant. So too officials, when they are fresh and inexperienced, obey their lord's orders very punctiliously and pay attention to the slightest detail, for they respect the oaths and penalties they take on themselves and fear to transgress accordingly. So they serve without greed or dishonesty and are spoken well of by all their clan.

But after they have been in office a long time they are apt to presume on people's acquiescence and get a high opinion of themselves, so that they do uncivil things they would never have done previously. And further, when they were new to office they would just touch and send back presents that were given them as the oath of the service requires, or should there be some special reason why they must receive them, before long they would make a return of equal value. However, after a while, a gradual, covetous spirit begins to arise in them, and while still declaring that they will take nothing and making an honest appearance, it is somehow made known that this is only a blind and their apparent scruples are soon overcome so that they accept these presents, and as a return favor cannot help robbing the government and giving partial decisions. And this defilement is just like the dirty color of a white garment, but where they differ is that this dirt can be washed away with lye, whereas the stain on a man's heart gets so ingrained that it can hardly be removed. And if a garment is washed two or three times a year it is enough, but a man's heart has to be continually cleansed and scoured and rinsed, sleeping and waking, every day in the year without remission, and even then it is easily soiled. And just as lye and practice of using it are needed for garments, so they are also for cleansing the hearts of samurai. And the practice here is that of the three principles of Loyalty, Duty, and Valor, while the lye must vary according to the nature of the dirt. For some will yield to that of fidelity and some to that of constancy, and though you may apply loyalty or duty there is some dirt that is so ingrained that it will not be washed out even then. But if to these things be added valor and intense application to their use then the defilement can be removed entirely. And this is the most profound secret of the purification of the samurai heart.

Borrowed and Stolen Authority

A samurai in service may be said to borrow his master's authority and also to rob him of it. And similarly his lord may lend it to him or let him steal it. When a retainer holds an important office, if he is young or of low rank he may be embarrassed by social customs or the current fashion and have to carry out his duties under the aegis of his master's authority. He thus holds it temporarily for his lord's advantage. This is borrowed authority, and if with its assistance he carries out his lord's intentions and benefits the people and renders it up again, he will have used it rightly in doing his duty with proper circumspection. But if, when he finds his comrades and also outsiders treating him with respect and addressing him as "Your Excellency" and "Your Honor" and so on, he becomes greedy of dignity and loath to part with it, then he may be described as one who steals it.

And regarding the other aspect of a lord lending his authority and giving his prestige to retainers, we find that in ancient times great nobles and famous commanders did this to a certain extent. And when they should have required this authority to be given back when the task was finished, sometimes from an easygoing nature they allowed it to be kept for some time, and then some incident arose that made it difficult to get it back except by paying a price for it. Here their retainers certainly robbed them of their authority. This is not only a great disgrace to a lord but causes him great damage. For if retainers get too much power, that of their master is thereby decreased, and if people come to think they can get what they want by honoring the vassal because he controls all access to the lord they will only think of getting into his good graces and regard the lord as of secondary importance, so that the benevolent relations of master and retainer will disappear and loyal samurai will become conspicuous by their absence.

Then, should some emergency arise, there will be no good men left to deal with it. Moreover, not only the outside retainers but those in personal attendance on the lord, as well as those in some quiet offices, will be oppressed by the authority of such a person, so that they will shrink in on themselves, and this also is not good for their lord. For they will say nothing about things they ought to notice, but only regret it in their hearts and grumble privately to their friends without anybody standing up and reporting it to their master. So the arbitrary conduct and partiality of the offender and the extent of his honor and glory remain unknown to his lord who only thinks well of all he does and thus by negligence brings about great misfortune. And the incapacity to know what people are is generally condemned as unfitting anyone to be a lord or commander.

Moreover, a man of this sort who cares nothing what his lord thinks is not likely to be sensitive to the opinion of his comrades. He will favor the little officials and give those who are his friends and acquaintances fees and bribes not of his master's property while taking their return presents for himself, and when he entertains his guests he has the fish and liquor and cakes brought from his lord's kitchen. So acting on the principle that what is my lord's is mine and what is mine is my own, he weakens his master's estate and causes him great loss. Think over all this very deeply therefore and remember always to be humble and suppress all pretensions when granted any privilege by your lord, so that nothing may dim the brightness of his glory. As the ancient saying has it, "The loyal retainer does not realize his own existence but only that of his lord."

On Tax Extortion

For a samurai in service the duties connected with the lord's exchequer are the most difficult. Because with but ordinary knowledge and ability it is a great problem how to do well for one's master without causing some hardship to the other retainers, not to speak of the farmers in the country and the citizens in the castle town. If you think only of your lord's interests, the lower people will have much to put up with, and if you try only to make their lot comfortable, your master will not be so well off, so there is sure to be some deficiency somewhere. And then, however clever and sagacious a samurai may be by nature, the disease of covetousness is easy to catch, and if he has to make arrangements to raise money for his lord's household and other expenses and has control of it, he may become consequential and luxurious and scheme to embezzle his lord's money, to build houses and collect curios and make an elegant appearance. This is the sort known as a thieving retainer.

Again, there is the official who makes a new system different from that of the former lord, asserting that it is for his master's benefit, without caring what hardship it causes his colleagues, and makes the citizens of the castle town pay higher dues, and levies larger land taxes on the farmers, only thinking of getting bigger amounts of revenue in the immediate future without any regard for people's comfort. Also he may deceive incompetent councillors and elders and chiefs of departments so that they agree to grant him improper increases in salary and rewards. But should these new regulations prove unworkable and ineffective, he will represent them as really planned by these councillors and chiefs, and so avoid punishment by sheltering behind their backs. And this sort is known as the tax-extorting retainer.

Now as to the previously mentioned thieving retainers, though they make away with their lord's substance in a way unworthy of a samurai and pervert justice accordingly, when heaven's punishment falls on them and the fact is made manifest by their personal ruin, when they are themselves overthrown, the matter is ended, for the people are no longer oppressed and the trouble in the administration and loss to the province also ceases. But the tax-extorting official produces a much more extensive injury and so it is more difficult to repair. For damage to the administration of the country is the greatest possible crime even if personal greed and peculation are not involved. Therefore do the sages of old declare that it is better to have a thieving official than a tax-extorting one. And though for a samurai there can be nothing worse than to gain the reputation of a peculator, the ancients condemn the extortioner more. So if the thief is punished by beheading, the extortioner ought to be crucified. This may have been the judgment of former times, but at the present day, since the actions of both may be regarded as the same, namely feathering their nest under the pretense of working for their lord's benefit, both are considered as equally heinous criminals. And for such a great offence it is difficult to say what penalty is adequate.

On Becoming a Thief

Small retainers serving under a guard captain or superintendent have to put up with being attentive to their various superiors and at the same time tolerant of the unequal qualities of their comrades. But should they have the good fortune to be promoted and given charge of a company themselves they should be sympathetic and considerate to those under them while also fulfilling their duty to their lord. It is perhaps unnecessary to say that they should not be partial or sycophants, but if in course of time they should rise to the positions of guard captain or superintendent, their former attitude is apt to change. For instance, Sakuma, vassal of Oda, and Uozumi, vassal of Hashiba, were examples of men who were admirable when they were humble samurai, but who deteriorated when they rose to high office and so were discarded by their lords and ruined.

Laziness

A samurai in service, as I said in the first chapter, must be one who lives for today but cares nothing for tomorrow, so that if he does what he has to do day by day, with zeal and thoroughness, so that nothing at all is left undone, he has no reason to feel any reproach or regret. But troubles arise when people rely on the future and become lazy and indolent and let things slide, putting off quite urgent affairs after a lot of discussion, not to speak of less important ones, in the belief that they will do just as well the next day. They push off this onto one comrade and blame another for that, trying to get someone to do it for them, and if there is no one to assist, they leave it undone so that before long there is a big accumulation of unfinished jobs. And this is a mistake that comes from relying on the future against which one must be very definitely on one's guard. For instance, on whatever day of the month is your fixed day to go on guard, you must calculate the time it will take you on the way from your house and allow for the length of the day, so that you are ready to take over duty just a little before the actual hour. For some silly fellows waste time by having a smoke when they ought to be starting, or chat with their wives or children, and so leave their house late and then have to hurry so that they do not recognize people they pass in the street. And when they do get to their destination, they are all covered with perspiration and playing their fans even in the cold weather, and then have to make some plausible excuse for their lateness on account of some very urgent business they had to do. When a samurai has to go on guard at his lord's castle he never ought to be late for any private reason. And if one man takes care to be a little early and then has to wait a bit for a comrade who is late, he should not squat down and yawn, neither should he hurry away when his time is up as though reluctant to be in his lord's mansions, for these things do not look at all well.

On the Road

When in the course of crossing a river or taking a ferry on a journey, two daimyos meet and a dispute starts between their respective retainers, and their comrades join in so that a general quarrel ensues, whether the lords themselves will be involved in it or not depends on how the matter is handled. And if both of them are so involved it may be difficult to settle it. And remember that it is from below that trouble arises, and when you travel with your lord, be very careful to look well after not only yourself but your comrades too, and adjure everybody down to the lowest to make sure that nothing unreasonable occurs.

And when you are escorting your lord on foot in Edo and meet another daimyo on the road, should the young samurai in front exchange words and come to blows, you must at once be on the alert to get your master's spears from the spear-bearer and stand by him and see how matters go. And should it be impossible to keep the peace and all the retainers have to draw their blades and enter the fray, you must at once bring your lord's horse up to the side of his

palanquin and help him to mount, and then un-
sheathe his spear and hand it to him, at the same
time being ready to draw your own sword and
hold your own.

And when you accompany your lord to an enter-
tainment, should anything untoward happen while
he is there and it appears that there may be a disturbance in the chamber, go to the porch, sword in
hand, and announce to the attendants, "I am So-and-
so, a retainer of Lord So-and-so, and as things seem
rather uproarious within, I feel a bit anxious about
my lord and so I have ventured thus far." Then
perhaps the attendants will reply, "We don't think
there is anything serious, though it is natural you
should be anxious, but as your lord is in no danger,
pray set your mind at ease," and you can report it
to your comrades. And that being so, everyone will
be delighted to hear it. Then you should ask the
attendant to find out if your lord will receive you,
and after you have seen him at once take your leave.

Showing One's Feelings

A samurai retainer who has done some special
service to his lord and considers it something ex-

traordinary, while perhaps others think so too and praise him, should understand that the matter may not appear quite the same to the lord himself. And even if he does feel moved inwardly there may be something else about it that offends him. And so if the retainer does not get any reward, and thinks his merit is overlooked, he may be dissatisfied and show what he feels by complaining continually about his lord's ingratitude, which is, it need hardly be said, the error of one who does not appreciate what service is.

Now the samurai of the civil war period were in the field innumerable times in their day and risked their lives freely for their lords and commanders but they did not talk about their merit or their valiant deeds. And peacetime service is merely shuffling about on the mats, rubbing the backs of the hands, and fighting battles with three inches of tongue for better or worse, and certainly nothing like risking one's life in war. But whether in peace or war it is the duty of samurai to serve in just the same spirit of loyalty. And whether what they do is anything special or praiseworthy or not, is for their lord to judge. It is enough that they resolve to do their duty properly, and they are not called upon to express any feelings of discontent.

Loyal to Death

A samurai in service is under a great debt to his lord and may think that he can hardly repay it except by committing *junshi* and following him in death. But that is not permitted by law, and just to perform the ordinary service at home on the mats is far from desirable. What then is left? A man may wish for an opportunity to do something more outstanding than his comrades, to throw away his life and accomplish something, and if he resolutely makes up his mind to do something of this sort it is a hundred times preferable to performing *junshi*. For so he may become the savior, not only of his lord, but of all his fellow retainers both small and great, and thus become a personage who will be remembered to the end of time as a model samurai possessing the three qualities of Loyalty, Faith, and Valor. Now there is always an evil spirit that haunts the family of a person of rank. And the way he curses that family is in the first place by causing the death by accident or epidemic disease of some young samurai among the hereditary councillors or elders who has the three virtues of a warrior and who promises to be of great value in the future as a support to his lord, as well as a benefit to all the clan, and whose loss is therefore a severe blow. Thus when Amari Saemon, commander of the samurai to Takeda Shingen, fell from his horse and was killed while quite young, that was the doing of the vicious spirit of Takasaki Danjō, who had long haunted that house. In the second place this evil spirit will enter into the person of one of the councillors or elders or samurai in attendance whom the lord most trusts and favors so that he may delude the lord's mind and seduce him into the ways of injustice and immorality.

Now, in thus leading his lord astray this samurai may do so in six different ways. First, he may prevent him from seeing or hearing anything and contrive that the others in attendance cannot state their views, or, even if they can, that they are not adopted, and generally manage so that his master regards him alone as indispensable and commits everything to his keeping. Secondly, if he notices that any of the samurai about the household seem promising and likely to be useful to their lord he will so work things that he is transferred somewhere else and kept away from his master, and that connections of his own, or men who agree with him and are subservient and respectful and never oppose him, are the only ones permitted to be about the lord. Thus he prevents his master from knowing anything about the extravagant and domineering way he lives. Thirdly, he may persuade his lord to take a secondary consort on the plea that he has not enough descendants to ensure the succession, and procure damsels for this purpose without any enquiry into what family they come from as long as they are good to look at. And he will collect dancers and players on the *biwa* and *samisen* and assure his lord that they are essential to divert him and dispel his boredom. And even a lord who is by nature clever and energetic is apt to be led astray by feminine fascinations, much more than one who is born lacking in these qualities. And then his discrimination will depart from him and he will think only of amusement, becoming more and more addicted to it, so that eventually he will be entirely given up to dancing and gaiety, inevitably followed by drinking parties at all times of the day and night. So he will come to spend all his time in the ladies' apartments without a thought for official and administrative business, and hating even the idea of an interview with his councillors on these subjects. Therefore, everything remains in the hands of the one evil councillor, and day by day his power increases, while all the others become mere nonentities with lips compressed and shrinking mien, and so the whole household goes from bad to worse. In the fourth place, it follows that under these circumstances, as everything is kept secret, expenses increase and income has to be augmented, so that the old regulations are done away with and new ones enacted, and a spy put in there and someone censured there and allowances cut down, so that the lower ranks are in great straits without anyone caring in the least about it, and all so that their lord may have plenty and live in the lap of luxury. So that, though they do not say anything about it publicly, the greatest discontent is rife among all the retainers, and before long there is none who is single-heartedly loyal to his lord. In the fifth place, though a daimyo is one who should never be anything but experienced in the Way of the Warrior, since the evil councillor is not likely to care anything about it in an age of peace and quiet such as this, there will be no interest at all in military matters and no inspections of the armed forces. And everyone in the household will be quite pleased to fall in with this attitude, and none will trouble about military duties or make proper provisions for weapons and supplies, and be perfectly content to let things alone and just make do for the present. So nobody would think, seeing the condition of the house now, that their ancestors had been warriors of great renown, and should some crisis supervene and find them unprepared, there would be nothing but flurry and confusion and nobody would know what to do. In the sixth place, when the lord is thus addicted to pleasure, drink, and dalliance, he will grow more and more wayward till his health becomes affected. All his retainers will be dispirited and lacking in sincerity, merely living from one day to the next and without any guidance from above, and eventually something may happen to the lord through the influence of this evil spirit.

This man who is at the bottom of it all, this vengeful enemy of his master and evil genius of his house, will be cursed by all the clan no doubt, but even so there will be nothing for it but that some nine or ten of them concert together to accuse him and bring him to judgment by a war of argument without soiling their hands. But in that case the affair cannot be cleared up without making it public, and the lord and his house will be brought up for examination, and then matters may become more serious and end in sentence being passed upon them by the shogun's government. And in all ages, when a daimyo has been unable to manage his affairs and has been disciplined by the government, the result has been that his house has come to an end. As the proverb has it, "When you straighten the horn you kill the ox, and when you hunt the rats you burn the shrine," so when the lord's house is ruined, his retainers are discharged and lose their livelihood. Therefore it is best to seize this great rascal of a councillor who is the evil spirit of the house and either stab him through or cut off his head whichever you prefer, and so put an end to him and his corrupt practices. And then you must straightway commit *seppuku* yourself. Thus there will be no open breach or lawsuit or sentence and your lord's person will not be tainted, so that the whole clan will continue to live in security and there will be no open trouble in the empire. And one who acts thus is a model samurai who does a deed a hundredfold better than *junshi,* for he has the three qualities of Loyalty and Faith and Valor, and will hand down a glorious name to posterity.

Matters Literary and Aesthetic

Though Bushido naturally implies first of all the qualities of strength and forcefulness, to have this one side only developed is to be nothing but a rustic samurai of no great account. So a samurai ought certainly to be literate, and, if he has time, should take up verse-making or Teaism to a certain extent. For if he does not study he will not be able to understand the reasons of things either past or present. And however worldlywise or sagacious he may be, he will find himself greatly handicapped at times for want of learning. For if you have a general understanding of the affairs of your own country and of foreign lands and carefully consider the three principles of time and place and rank, and follow the best course, you are not likely to make many mistakes in your calculations. And that is why I assume that a samurai should be studious. But if he makes bad use of his knowledge and grows opinionated and looks down on the illiterate as not all there, and if he becomes a worshiper of everything foreign and thinks nothing any good if it is not Chinese, and is so prejudiced that he cannot perceive that a thing may be unsuitable for Japan at the present time, good though it may be in theory, then I say his learning is too much of a good thing. With this in view he should study.

Again, verse-making is a custom of our country and great soldiers in all ages have been distinguished in it, so that even a humble retainer will do well to go in for it and try his hand at a clumsy verse on occasion. But anyone who gets entirely absorbed in it and neglects his ordinary duties will become soft in mind and body and lose all martial qualities and look like nothing but a courtier-samurai. Particularly, if you get too fond of these short *haikai* verses that are now so fashionable, you may easily get into the way of being glib-tongued and witty and smart even in the company of grave and reserved colleagues, and though this may be amusing in society at the present time it is an attitude samurai ought to avoid. Then, as for *cha-no-yu,* from the days of the Kyoto shoguns it has been very much the diversion of the military class, and even though you are not yourself a great enthusiast yet, you are likely to be invited to take part in it and be a fellow-guest with people of high degree, so that you ought to know at least how to enter the Tea-room and its precincts properly, how to view arrangements and processes intelligently, and how to eat the meal and drink the tea correctly. And to obtain this knowledge of the rules of the procedure it is advisable to take some lessons from a Tea-master. Again, the Tea-room is a place very profitable for the enjoyment of retirement and tranquillity far removed from ostentation and luxury, so that even in the grounds of the wealthy and of officials you find these reed-thatched huts with their pillars of natural wood and their rafters of bamboo set in what seems to be a solitary mountain valley with their bare simplicity of plain lattice window, bamboo blind, and rustic wicket gate and entrance. And the tea vessels and other utensils are equally without any meretricious ornament, but of clean and reticent form entirely eschewing the impurities of everyday life, a spirit which if cultivated is, I think, of great assistance in sweetening the Way of the Warrior. So it is no bad thing for anyone to make a place for *cha-no-yu* if he has only pictures by present-day artists and tea utensils by modern potters and an earthenware tea-kettle so that it is all quite inexpensive and in accordance with the austere style of Teaism. But in all things the simple is very apt to become complicated, and luxury may show itself, and if, for instance, when you see someone else's Ashiya kettle you feel disgusted with your own earthenware one, you will soon come to want all your utensils to be things of value. Then you will cultivate an eye for a bargain and go in for connoisseurship, so that you can pick up a fine piece for a small sum. Then, if you see anything very attractive at anybody's house you will importune him for it or else want to make an exchange for it with, of course, the intention of getting the best of it yourself. This kind of thing is no better than the nature of a huckster or broker and degrades the Way of the Warrior to that of the mere tradesman. It is a very bad fault, and rather than practice this kind of Teaism, it is better to know nothing about it at all, and to remain ignorant of even how to drink powder tea. For it is preferable to appear a little boorish than to spoil the quality of Bushido.